60

SECOND
COACH

Maximizing Talent, Passion and Cause in 60 Seconds

by Frank Keck

The 60-Second Coach

I believe that you can change your life by changing how you think. You can help others, whether they be employees, customers, or those closer to you, by helping them change how they think.

We just happen to call this---COACHING.

I started out as a coach when a client of mine asked me if I would coach her. I agreed to do this not knowing what it was really about.

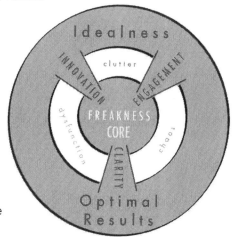

When I worked for Dale Carnegie back in the 90s, we coached people through each session---teaching them how to think on their feet and how to communicate to the world around them.

While I did not really think of it at the time, I was getting some world class experience in coaching people to higher performances.

When I started coaching my first coachee, I found myself asking lots of questions, because I was curious, and frankly I had no idea how to help her fix her mess (her word).

After about fifteen minutes on our first session, this first client looked at me and told me what a great coach I was, that she now saw things very differently---all because I asked a bunch of questions so that I could better understand what was going on.

I learned that a coach's job is to help his or her people achieve success, by helping them see themselves having success, by helping them to think DIFFERENTLY than they are right now. The ways in which you get people to think differently are various, and it is what this book is all about.

My coaching model is the center of this entire book. You start by helping your people develop a core, a solid foundation, their FREAKNESS if you will.

To this end, there are specific coaching activities to help you help them develop their Core.

After the core is established, you need to determine where you are going, your Optimal Performance. This is the outer ring in the model and there are specific coaching activities to help you help them determine their Optimal Performance and WHY it is important.

Then you have the roads, the paths from the core to the optimal results. These pathways are what I believe each of us must focus on in order to reach our nirvana.

Path one, Clarity: Clarity is having a mutual understanding from two or more people (sometimes the person that needs the most clarity is you). There are 12 coaching activities that you can use to help gain greater clarity for you, your people, your team.

Path two, Engagement: How do we get our people engaged, and how do we keep them engaged? There are 13 activities that will help you to get and to keep your people engaged to help them move forward, closer to their goals.

Path three, Innovation: How to do things faster, better, cheaper. Constant improvement. Again, there are 13 activities to help be more innovative in what ever it is that you are doing.

There are also 13 activities that focus on CORE and Idealness. That is a total of 51 activities in this book. That is ONE activity PER WEEK for almost an entire year. Think about that, a fresh idea and coaching activity for an entire year. Best of all, you do NOT necessarily have to do these in order. Mix them up, try them in different orders. Keep it fresh for both of you. Just have a plan, and fit the tools to the plan.

My goal is to help you to think differently when it comes to developing your people. I hope I have succeeded to this end, with this book.

Now, go and change the world!

Frank Keck
December 8, 2014

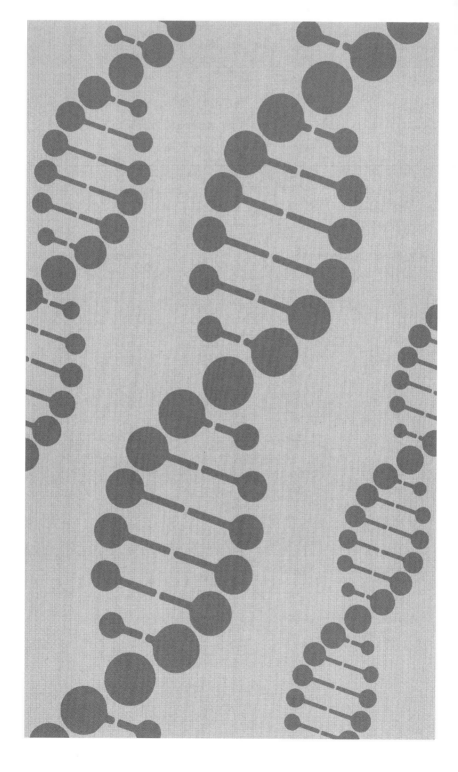

Chapter 1

CORE
DEVELOPMENT

Your essence, your DNA, why you exist, a combination of beliefs, purpose and causes. Your CORE includes your driving force and your three primary values.

CORE Tip #1:

Start a CULT

Doing research on creating a positive culture, I had a realization: culture starts with a CULT. A cult is defined as a group that shares values and beliefs. Share with your team what you value and what you believe. Ask them to share their values and beliefs as well. Start with the values and beliefs that apply to your work. See how that goes and then share accordingly. Some groups will want to expand their sharing, others not so much. Make space for those who want to share and those who don't want to share. Create an environment of trust, sharing, and caring, and you are on your way towards creating a CULT.

Now, go and change the world.

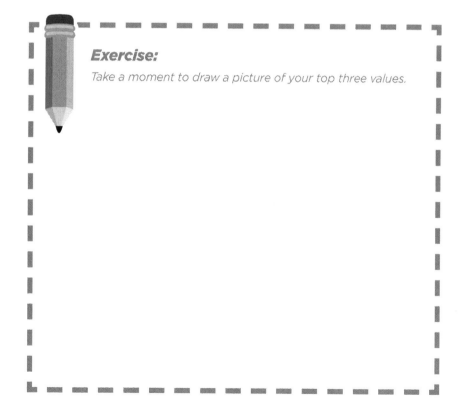

Exercise:

Take a moment to draw a picture of your top three values.

CORE Tip #2:

Share Slogans or Mottos

I yam what I yam.

Just a humble shoe shine boy, little ole me . . .

The Golden Rule

These are just a few slogans and mottos that guide people's lives (to be fair, the first is from Popeye and the second from UnderDog and the third is found in every one of the world's great traditions).

Most people have a slogan or motto by which they live their lives. Spend time getting to know what your employees' mottos or slogans are. This will go a long way towards helping you see things from their perspectives. For example, if an employee lives by The Golden Rule, i.e., "Do unto others as you would have them do unto you," and the employee doesn't like himself or herself, then you know why he or she treats others so badly.

Have a 60-second conversation. What is her motto? What is his slogan? Where did it originate? What does it mean? How does it color their worlds? Share your motto or slogan with them; it will help them to understand where you are coming from.

Now, go and change the world . . . (one of MY slogans).

CORE Tip #3:

A Force to Be Reckoned With

Think about this: You have a team of people which is a force to be reckoned with . . . in a positive perspective. They are all on fire to achieve the desired goals of the team. You don't have to motivate them on a daily basis, because they are self-motivated. They are en fuego. They are on a mission. How can you get your people to be a Force? By getting them to identify their own Driving Force. Your Driving Force is a combination of your passion, your cause, your mission, what gets you out of bed in the morning. Help your team to figure that out; really encourage them to think about the answers to those questions; then wrap it up in a nice, brief sentence. Brief sentences are easier to remember . . . for both you and for them.

Once they have determined their Driving Forces, with your support and encouragement, have a conversation with them about how the Driving Force of the team is in alignment with their personal Driving Force. Now you have driven, aligned employees. You are building a team that is a Force to Be Reckoned with!

Now, go and change the world . . . and use the Force!

Cartoons Breed Success
- or at Least Understanding

Did you watch cartoons as a kid? What was your favorite? Why was that your favorite? What was it that you most liked about the cartoon? My favorite was Mighty Mouse, his slogan was "Here I am to save the day." He was all about helping others with his super powers.

I have been using this exercise in my workshops and conferences for years for one simple reason: it helps me get to know you and what you value. You see, the character you select, and what you like most about them is really how you see yourself. So for me, I see myself as a superhero helping others by saving the day, however that may be. This exercise is a bit right-brained, nonsensical if you will, and it will bring a smile to MOST people's faces. It also helps you to understand a little more how your people see themselves. Heck, it will help you to see how you see yourself!

Now, go and change the world . . . one yuck at a time!

Share Your Values Proposition

Steven Covey introduced the world to the term "values proposition" in his best selling book *The Seven Habits of Highly Effective People*. Most of us have heard of this concept. How many of us have actually put it into practice? A much smaller number to be sure.

The concept is to create a work environment based on one's values. In order to do this, one must first IDENTIFY his or her values and then COMMUNICATE with his/her people what these values are, as well as get input from the people as to what THEIR values are.

Why would you want to do this? When you share your values, your people have a better understanding of what drives you, of what is important to you. I hear salespeople talk about providing "extra value" to their customers, yet when you ask them what it is their customers value, they don't have an answer. How can you provide more of something you can't identify?

Write down some of your daily actions, behaviors and habits. Start with about 20. Then make a second column and write down what belief drives the behavior. WHY do you do each activity? If you are honest with yourself, you will start to see a pattern of your most important values. WE ALWAYS HAVE TIME FOR WHAT IS IMPORTANT!

Next, ask your people about one of their daily activities. Then ask them to tell you WHY they think they do it, what the belief behind the action is. Do this each day with them until you have at least ten different values. Then you can start to pare them down to their top three. Now you have shared your values with them, and they have shared theirs with you.

You will find this provides a much deeper level of understanding (clarity) and engagement (buy in).

Now, go and change the world . . . one value at a time.

The Making of True Value

We talk about providing our internal customers (our employees) with added value. How do we do that?

First of all, you must know WHAT their values are. What is important to them? What do they make time for in their lives? Play to their values. How can you provide MORE of what they yearn for?

Now, if what they yearn for is not working, then perhaps you need to re-evaluate your hiring processes, or perhaps that person's seat on the bus. Barring that scenario, provide value to your employees first, then ask for them to provide value back. It works! How do you do this in one minute? Ask them. What are your three top values in life? How do those values play out in your daily life? How can I help you to get more of that here at work?

Watch them. Watch what they do. We always have time for what is important to us, for what we value. Make a list of things they do and then WHY you think they do those things. If you don't want to guess, take a 60-second CHAT opportunity and ask, "I noticed you did this the other day (this being a specific action or activity or behavior). I was just wondering what drove you to do that? What is the importance of it to you?"

Be careful. You don't want to come across as condescending or accusatory or negative. You want to come across as curious, caring, and wanting to help them optimize their performance. Listen to what they say. Ask follow up questions until you feel like you understand where they are coming from. Take mental notes and add it to your written file on each employee so you have notes to refer back to. Your employees are important. Learn what drives them, then coach to those values.

Now, go and change world . . . by creating True Value!!

CORE Tip #7:

Innerview

When does 1 = 10? Now. Let me introduce you to a tool---ONE tool that has 10 parts. Since this series is the 60-second Coach, each of these questions will be one 60-second coaching session.

The idea of the Innerview came from my days at Dale Carnegie Training back in the late '80's. The idea is to find what is at the core of someone by asking some specific questions. Each of these questions, when answered by your employee, will shine a light into his/her values and beliefs. As you listen to each answer, ask yourself: what does this tell me about this person, or what value drives that answer?

For example, the question: If you could have dinner with any three people, living or dead, who would they be and why? Answers will tell you which people they value in their lives, what contributions those three people have made to their lives, or why they would want to spend time with them. It tells you what they value. If they list a family member, it probably means they value family. If they name Einstein, they most likely value creativity or seek intelligence. If they select Oprah (a favorite among women by the way), it tells you they value equality and role models of people who have done incredible things and stood up for themselves.

Here are the 10 Innerview questions. You do NOT have to do them in order. Do only one per coaching session.

1. If you could change one thing about yourself, what would you change?

2. If you could change one thing about your job, or the company, what would you change?

3. What are your three greatest passions in life?

4. What do you do to get away from it all and relax?

5. If you could have dinner with any three people, living or dead, who would they be and WHY?

6. What are your three greatest successes in life so far?

7. If you left tomorrow, what would people miss the most about you?

8. If you could teach the people of the world three things, what would those three things be?

9. What three things do you want to accomplish before you leave the earth?

10. What is the best advice you can give your son or daughter? (If they have no children, then a child in their life who is important to them.)

This exercise will tell you much about them. Be confidential with their answers. Be genuine in your conversations with them. When they answer, know that it may be difficult for them. Give them some time. Also, allow some time for a discussion to follow their answer. After all, we want to support them and the things that are IMPORTANT to them.

Now, go and change the world . . . one Innerview at a time.

IF YOU COULD TEACH THE PEOPLE OF THE WORLD THREE THINGS, WHAT WOULD THOSE THREE THINGS BE?

Would You Rather . . .

Have you ever played that game? It's a game of options. You're given a choice between two different things from which you have to choose. Some are serious; some are silly; most are pretty thought provoking.

(Would You Rather . . . ? Extra Extremely Extreme Edition: More than 1,200 Positively Preposterous Questions to Ponder by Justin Heimberg and David Gomberg (Jul 16, 2012)---Kindle eBook)

This is a simple and fun tool to get to know your employees in a non-threatening manner. Ask them one question at a time, then talk about the answers. It's an out-of-the-box type exercise that will give you so much insight as well as keep them on their toes.

One of my favorites, "Would you rather vacuum every room in the Empire State Building or wash every window?" What a choice! Personally, I would rather vacuum every room---kinda have this thing about heights.

WOULD YOU RATHER BE RIGHT OR BE HAPPY?

What does that answer tell you? 1. I have a fear of heights and 2. I am probably not a HUGE risk taker. Seek answers to help you in your quest of optimal performance for your people.

Now, go and change the world . . . or move to Mars---which would you rather?

Chapter 2:

IDEALNESS

Making the most of what you have and what you believe, maximizing talent, passion and cause. It is there for the experiencing. You just have to CHOOSE to live a RICHER life.

Define Success

What is success to you? Success is a very personal thing. Personal from the standpoint that it is defined differently by everyone. Each of us has our version or definition of what success is . . . for ourselves, for our families, for others. One way to ensure your people are successful is to know what their definition of success is.

So ask them. Have a conversation, listen, write it down. Ask them how you can help them to find that success. Have regular success progress meetings. Let them know you want them to be successful.

Then share with them what your definition is . . . both for yourself and for them. Talk about what your definition of success for them entails and how you can come to a mutual understanding to achieve both versions of success.

Meet on a regular basis. I would suggest once per quarter. Check on the progress that both of you are making towards success.

Now, go and change the world . . . by being more successful!

Eight Areas of Focus for Idealness:

IDEALNESS Tip #2:

Determine Career Ambitions

What do you want to do with your life? Where do you want to be in three years? Two very popular questions we ask people when they are interviewing for a position with us . . . and then it kind of goes by the wayside. Their answers are VERY important. Their answers give you insight to where they want to head in their career. With that information, you can help them to achieve their career goals . . . you become GOALED-EN! You show them how much you care by helping them get what they want.

Start with a brief 60-second CHAT: Where do you want to be in three years? Listen to the answer, then ask a follow up question for discussion at the next CHAT. A follow up question such as how do you see yourself getting there or how do you see this job/company helping you achieve that goal? Encourage the person to take some time and think about the question. Ensure him/her that you truly want to help.

One employee told me he wanted to be a chef in three years (we were working for Circuit City at the time). Not only a different company . . . but a different profession altogether. Rather than freak out, I told him, "Cool, Chad, I would love to help you get there. Take some time to think about how you want to get there and how I can help. I'd be happy to help you put together a plan."

We put together a plan and Chad became my most motivated employee. He motivated others on his team and took his team to new levels. It was incredible! We would follow up on his progress toward his career goals at least once per quarter. I wanted to be sure he knew I was behind him and supported him. After a few quarters, he started coming to me and saying, "I think it's time for a career status update. Got a few minutes?"

Now, go change and the world . . .

What would you do if you could not fail?

There are NO guarantees in life. But what if there were? What would you do if you could not fail? What would you try? What would you change? How would your life be different?

Falling down is part of life; it's how humans learn. My one-year old Addie just learned how to walk (and is now learning to run). As she started to learn, I would hold her hands to help her balance. Then, she would take steps. Each time we practiced, she went a little further, got a little braver, bolder, more confident. Finally, she wanted to do it without my assistance at all. She fell . . . many times. She always got back up. Why? Because she had a burning desire to walk. A passion to learn something new. A desire to be more independent. My job, as her dad, is to give her support, to give her encouragement, to dust her off when she falls, give her a smile and a hug, tell her I love you and let her start all over again.

Kids learn more by the age of five than we learn the entire rest of our lives. Why is that? I believe it is because they are curious and persistent. They have not LEARNED how to have low self esteem or how to quit.

What if you treated your employees like a five-year old? What if you consistently encouraged them to fall down . . . and then helped them get up and learn from it. Not by doing things FOR them, but by helping them do things for THEMSELVES. Develop their abilities to be independent. Empower them. Build trust in one another. With you coaching them, falling down becomes a learning opportunity. Imagine what they can accomplish!

Now, go and change the world . . . try falling down!

I Want

This post was going to be about helping your people create a bucket list. A bucket list is a list of things you want to do before you die. Then I was talking to my wife Rachel and she suggested that instead of focusing on doing things before you die, create a list of things you want WHILE YOU ARE ALIVE! Hmmm, a different focus to be sure. So I went about creating my "I Want" list. I wondered how this list would be different from my bucket list started several years ago. Here's what I found.

Many similar items . . . but the focus is all different. The focus now is on things I want to do to really live, to be more proactive . . . to make life more fulfilling. The items are more life giving and oddly enough, involve people more. They are things that bring me joy . . . as opposed to things that would be cool to do. There are still cool things to do on my list . . . and MOST of my "I Want" list consists of things that make me HAPPY, things that bring me JOY and FULFILLMENT.

Think about this, what would happen to your employees if you help them to create a mindset where they focus on happiness, joy and fulfillment? How would this impact them when they have to do things that don't fill them up or don't bring them joy? What I have found is by using this list, the people I coach have a bigger savings deposit, so when little things happen, they have more energy to draw from . . . the little energy sucking things that happen to us on a daily basis are not as big a deal because they have a reserve.

Coach your people to create "I WANT" lists. Then talk about the items on their lists and how you can help them fulfill it. Create your own list, share it with them.

Now, go and change the world . . . by focusing on wants!

Set SMART and POWERFUL Goals

Grab the GOLD. That's what goal setting and goal achieving can do for you and your employees. How often do your employees look at their goals? How well written are their goals? I have been teaching goal setting for many years now. Many people write down wishes, not goals. What is a wish? Something you'd like to have. What is a goal? A wish with specificity and a plan.

If you follow the SMART POWERFUL formula, it will help you to write goals that are more apt to get accomplished. Goals that are more powerful and smarter lead to better results.

While you cannot always set goals in one 60-second coaching session, this formula will give you a framework to talk to your employees about goal setting and achieving. It will give you a framework to help them stay on track and to know where they are in the pursuit of their wishes written with specificity . . . a.k.a. goals.

Specific: The more specific your goal is, the more likely it is to be accomplished. Generating more revenue . . . not a goal, a wish. Generating $50,000 more in sales in one calendar year is more specific.

Measurable: How will you know when you have achieved the goal? If you cannot measure it, then it is a wish.

Applicable: Does the goal apply to their life goals and their career goals?

Realistic: Is it even possible to achieve? If a goal is TOO hard to achieve, then it actually creates a negative response and demotivates the person.

Time Frame: What is the specific time frame for this goal to be accomplished? Also, what are the time frames in the steps of the goal?

SMART goals are pretty well known, now for the POWERFUL element. These steps will help get you through the challenging times of goal achievement.

Positive: Is your goal written in a positive rather than negative form?

Obstacles: What obstacles might you incur and what's the backup plan?

Win/win: Does your goal create a win/win situation?

Encompassing: Have you developed goals in all eight areas of life?

Rewards: What's in it for you? How will you celebrate once you've achieved your goal?

Fitting: Does your goal fit with all your other goals, as well as with your personal vision, mission and values?

Urgent: Is your goal something you sincerely care about? Is it something you urgently desire, not just a passing whim?

Level-up: Does your goal challenge you to take your game to the next level?

This framework gives many opportunities to have conversations with your people about their goals. It will also help you to write smarter, more powerful goals for yourself!

Now, go and change the world . . . one goal at a time!

Chapter 3:

CLARITY

Clarity is the ability to see where you are going, to have a target.
It also entails the ability to see where you are, to see what the
situation really is. Add the ability to communicate that clearly to
others and you have synchronicity.

CLARITY Tip #1:

Coaching Pact

Coaching will be a great ride full of ups and downs. Before you go on this ride together, make a commitment to one another.

Several years ago, I met one of my mentors, Melody. When she agreed to mentor me, she said that she would do it, but with a few conditions. Little did I know then, this was my first coaching pact The conditions were simple: be honest, listen to what she told me, and do my best. Pretty simple pact, actually. If I did that, Melody said that she would hold up her end, which was to give me positive, solid suggestions, always support me (which means telling me what I need to hear, not necessarily what I WANT to hear), and always to be there when I needed her.

Think about this: Would you go into a relationship, a long term relationship, without knowing anything about what the other person's expectations and aspirations were? Wouldn't you want to know what they expect from you so that you can deliver, and to make sure that their expectations are realistic? Same thing with the Coaching Pact. Expectations are the minimum acceptable performance. Aspirations are above and beyond the minimum.

It is a very simple form. First, what is it that they expect from you? Second, what is it that you expect from them? These two segments get the basics out of the way. Third, what are their aspirations of you? What is it that they hope you will do above and beyond the minimum? Fourth, what are your aspirations of them? What do you want to see them do above and beyond the minimum.

Make this a working pact and review it on a regular basis. Make adjustments: what is working and what is not working, what needs to be added or subtracted? Talk about the benefits to both of you.

Now, go and change the world . . . together.

Set CLEAR EXPECTATIONS

You know what you want, but do they? Before you shower them with your expectations, follow this simple formula:

Channel: Get on their communication channel (Social, Driver, Lover, Thinker).

Large Picture (outcome): Share with them the bigger picture of the subject.

Explicit: Share the details that they will need. This should be collaborative. This should include the desired end result, how it will get completed, when it will get completed, who will complete it, and what obstacles you anticipate. Also include the reward for completion. By doing this together, you will gain clarity and buy in.

Agree: Get their agreement on the details.

Reward: Share the agreed upon reward. Celebrate. Behavior rewarded is behavior repeated.

Now, go and change the world.

CHANNEL
LARGE PICTURE
EXPLICIT
AGREE
REWARD

Be FABulous

It's not about you. It is about them. In order to connect with your people, you have to talk their language. You want your people to buy what you are selling (do what you want them to do). In order to get that, you have to show them WII-FM (what's in it for me). They want to know WHY should I do this. People buy benefits, not facts. Managers talk in terms of facts, not benefits. Know what each of your employees wants from life and the job, then show them how what you need them to do will help them to reach their goals and voile, you have a motivated and inspired employee.

FAB is Fact and Benefit. Don't just give them a fact, give them the benefit too.

FACT:
We need you here on time.

BENEFIT:
People who count on you don't have to sit and wait for you so that they can start their jobs, resulting in more productivity, which means more profits, which means you can take that extra day off each month that you were requesting. Show them how their behavior can get them what they want

Now, go and change the world.

The GOAL-ed Standard

Is the term Gold Standards really a true statement? Can you get the Gold by sticking to the standards? Goals are important . . . Goals when achieved are . . . GOAL-ED. Now then, excuse my play on words here . . . it does make sense.

Many of us think that goals and standards are the same, when in fact they are very different.

Standards: The lowest acceptable performance. Standards apply to the position, and anyone with that particular position will have the same standards. Anything less is not acceptable. The standard is the baseline, it is what we want to perform higher than. Goals: Above and beyond the standard.

Goals apply to the individual, not the position. You may have five people with the same position. Each will have a shared set of standards, but they will have their own individual goals. This gives you some flexibility and freedom when it comes to leading and coaching. Coach people on both their performance compared to the standards and compared to their goals. Help people to understand these two concepts and how as a team you MUST focus on both.

Start setting goals with your people, ask them what they aspire to and then set some goals based on those aspirations.

Talk to your people about the standards of their job every week. Talk to them about their goals at least once per week and preferably daily. When you coach, use different tools to coach performances ABOVE the standard than BELOW the standard.

Now, go and change the world.

If You Only Expect and Don't Aspire, You Will Expire

Quick, what is the difference between an expectation and an aspiration? An expectation is defined as something you expect. Think about it though, when someone does something you expected, they have just fulfilled to the point of zero. They have not gotten ahead, they have not exceeded expectations. Your expectation is the minimum. That's what they did in your eyes . . . even if it took a monstrous effort on their part. They see victory, but you see only an average performance.

Aspiration, ambition, above the norm, above the expectation. When someone aspires to something, they WANT to achieve it. An expectation is something they HAVE to achieve. BIG difference. We need to have both in coaching and in life. Start talking about both, start setting targets in both. What is the **expectation**? What is the **aspiration** for the same event?

Here is an example. You want Joe to be on time. Your expectation is that Joe is in his chair, ready to start performing at 9am. That is the MINIMUM. Anything less . . . not acceptable. So Joe busts his hump to get to the office, ready to go by 9am. In his eyes, he has done a GREAT job, he has done what you have asked. Joe now has an expectation of you . . . PRAISE for his job well done.

Why praise the minimum you think? You don't praise Joe for fulfilling the expectation . . . heck, you shouldn't even have to tell him that, it is just expected! Now there is discord. Now there is miscommunication. Now there is conflict.

What if you talk to Joe about the expectation and the aspiration? The expectation is that you are in your chair, ready to start producing at 9am. Now, let's talk about what you would like to aspire to ABOVE and BEYOND that expectation. The aspiration must be a joint effort with MOST of it coming from them. You will need to talk about WHY they would want to aspire, what is the benefit to them, to you, to the organization or the team.

Take things one step further . . . talk about expectations and ASPIRATIONS. See how your people change their performances and their attitudes!

Now, go and change the world (expectation) or more (aspiration)!

Exercise:

Take a moment to draw a picture of what you aspire to in the next year.

500 Degrees-It's Hot (and Lonely) at the Top

Feedback is the food of success. Without feedback, you cannot continue to improve. Sometimes, we are afraid to get feedback. How do I know that? Because we don't ask for it. Why don't we ask for it? Perhaps we don't want to hear it because we are pretty sure it won't be good. Stop that. It is time to get some feedback. Some of it will be better than you think, some worse. You cannot improve what you do not acknowledge. You must lead by example. We want our people to listen to our feedback. It's time to get some from others. Many organizations have the 360 feedback tool. This can be a very valuable tool. I think we need more TARGETED feedback, so let me introduce you to the 500 Degree feedback formulator.

The 500 Degree Feedback Formulator helps you to get 100% input from 5 different people. Feedback on your strengths and weaknesses, opportunities and threats. Things they see and maybe you do . . . but maybe you don't. The point is you are getting pointed, pertinent feedback.

Think about five people that you would like to get feedback from. Here are some suggestions:

1. Someone you are coaching.

2. Someone who is coaching/mentoring you.

3. Someone who is a customer of yours. (a customer is defined as someone who uses your products or services, internally or externally)

4. Someone from a different part of your organization who does not report to you nor do you report to them.

5. Someone who knows you very well, who will be very open and honest with you . . . outside your work organization.

These are five different perspectives. Ask them the same questions, listen to their answers. What patterns are emerging? How will this help you to put together a strategic plan of improvement? Create a SWOT (Strengths, Weaknesses, Opportunities, Threats) analysis based on this feedback and then apply the 80/20 rule, focus 80% of your time and effort improving strengths and 20% improving weaknesses.

Here are some sample questions or you can come up with your own. The idea is to get feedback that will help you improve your performance:

1. What is it that I do best? Where have you seen this? How could I do this even better?

2. What is it that I am below standard at? Where have you experienced this? What can I do to improve this performance

3. What one thing could I stop doing that would improve my performance? Where have you seen me do this, how is this behavior impacting others?

4. What is one thing I should START doing and why? What benefits will this create and to whom?

There you have it. Do it all at once, or do them one at a time. Great feedback, 500 degrees!

Now, go and change the world!

CLARITY Tip #7:

Pareto was a Genius

The 80/20 rule, most of us have heard of it at one point or another. Business-consultant J.M. Juran who suggested the principle and named it after Italian economist Vilfredo Pareto, who observed in 1906 that 80% of the land in Italy was owned by 20% of the population; Pareto developed the principle by observing that 20% of the pea pods in his garden contained 80% of the peas.

How does this principle apply to your coaching? Most of the time, managers and coaches spend 80% of the time talking to their people about what is broken, what they are doing wrong and then telling them to go fix it. What we find is that this approach does not work.

In his best selling book, *Now, Break All the Rules,* Marcus Buckingham talks about a different approach with the 80/20 rule. 80% of your coaching should be to develop their strengths, 20% to improve their weaknesses.

Think about this. If you spend 80% of your time trying to fix something, that is time you are NOT spending on improving something they are already good at doing. Think about what you are good at doing. What if you could do MORE of what you are good at, more of what you LOVE to do, more of what ENERGIZES you? How much more would you get done? How much more positive would you be every day at work? How much better would your life be?

Spend 80% of your coaching time, coaching your people's strengths. Use the coaching tools for ABOVE the standard and help them continue to improve their strengths. Spend 20% of your coaching time coaching to improve weaknesses. You both will get far more from the coaching sessions than you get with the opposite approach.

Talk to your people about this approach. Talk about the benefits and the potential drawbacks and then try it for 60 days.

You both will be thrilled at how this improves both your relationship and performances!

Now, go and change the world . . . by focusing on strengths 80% of the time!

You Say Potato, I Say Not an Orange

Have you ever heard the phrase, "you say po-tay-toe, I say potah-toe"? The concept being that we say things differently and that is ok. A potato is still a potato, no matter how you say it. Let's take this concept one step further . . . how does this apply to life? The potato is still the potato, some of us see it one way . . . how it is similar to every other potato we have ever seen . . . and some of us realize, this potato is different . . . it is NOT an orange. What? Some people may be drawn to a potato because it is NOT an orange . . . it is different.

There are two categories to discover about yourselves. Similarities and Differences. Most of us see the world more through one than the other. People who are considered to be similarities people look at the world and see how things are the same. Differences people look at the world and see how things are different.

So you can both experience the same event and a similarities person would see it very differently than a differences person. The similarities person will see how things are the same. The differences person will see how things are different. This is very important when you are coaching. A similarities person wants to see how what you are suggesting is similar to things they know in their experiences. A differences person will want to see how things are different than what they have experienced before.

Start to pay attention to your people, do they compare things and see similarities or differences? How can this information better help you be a coach to them? How can this make your life better, easier? What adjustments do you want to make based on this information?

Now, go and change the world . . . or another orb circling the Sun.

Mind Your P's and Q's

"Mind your P's and Q's" is a saying that means to pay attention to the details. P's and Q's in coaching refers to People Quotient, your PQ. While your IQ measures your intelligence quotient, how intelligent you are, and your EQ measures your emotional intelligence, your PQ measures your people quotient, your people intelligence.

The concept here is simple. Have conversations with your people about their awareness of others. What things do they notice? How can that help them to better interact with other people?

Here are some things to talk with your people about to help them increase their PQ.

1. Cultural observations. What do you notice about other people's cultural behaviors and traditions? What is your perception of these behaviors and traditions?

2. Communication observations. What do you notice about how other people communicate? Are they big chunk or small chunk? Do they talk fast or slow, are they good listeners? How do they like to be communicated with?

3. Behavioral observations. What do you notice about other people's behaviors and tendencies. How does this impact you and how you interact with them?

There are many, many more observations, these are but a few to get started on increasing PQ.

Now, go and raise your awareness and change the world!

Just the Basics Ma'am

Remember Joe Friday from Dragnet? "Just the facts ma'am." That quote became a cultural iconic saying. Joe Friday was an LA police officer, and he would go to interview a victim or witness and all he wanted was the facts, not a bunch of emotions and excessive stuff. Just the facts, that's what he needed to get his job done. He said it in a low, monotone, deadpan voice.

The point of Joe Friday? Let's keep it basic, don't get fancy. Let's establish some basic elements of communication here.

I love that idea. Some basic elements of communication. To get your coaching and relationship going, or to perhaps improve your relationship or communication with your employee, just have BASIC conversations with them.

Background: Ask them questions about their background, their job, where they grew up, what things they have done in the past. Ask follow up questions to elaborate.

Achievements: Ask questions about what things they have achieved in their jobs and in their life. Ask follow up questions to find out more about their achievements. How did they do it, what did it feel like, what feedback did they get from it?

Share: Be sure to share this same information with them, a little bit at a time. The listening to sharing ration should be 80% listen, 20% share.

Interests: What kinds of things interest them? What do they do in their spare time? What is the most interesting part of their job? What is the least interesting? Why?

Comfortable: Pay attention to body language and facial expressions. Lead the way with your body language and your facial expressions.

Be sure to smile and be relaxed. What ever your body language says, they will take cues from subconsciously. So be sure to lead by example, relaxed and interested. Smile, smile, smile.

Now, go and change the world . . . one basic conversation at a time!

CLARITY Tip #11:

Employees are from Pluto

John Gray wrote a best selling book, *Men are from Mars, Women are from Venus*. The premise is that men and women communicate very differently, and for different reasons. In order to communicate effectively, you must understand more about the other person and how THEY communicate.

I think the same thing is true at work. Not only do men and women communicate differently, but managers and employees communicate differently. We (coaches and managers) see things one way, they see it another.

Think about it, have you ever wondered after watching an employee's performance, "what were they thinking"? You just have no idea what was running through their mind. Why? Because they are from Pluto and you aren't.

The coaching tip here is this . . . they are different, they are NOT you. So you have to figure out what is important to them. What is it that matters in their lives? What do they want out of life, what do they want out of their job?

The Pluto challenge: Find out the three most important things to your employee. One from work, one from personal life, and one important experience from their past that continues to color their perspective. How can you help them to achieve these three things? If you were driven by these three things, how might you think?

Here is an example. I was coaching a client, Sarah, and she told me that her dad and her were very close when she was a kid. Now I did not just out and ask her this, I listened. Many times, Sarah would share something with me and when I asked her where she learned that, she would say from her father. When we talked a little further, she shared that her dad was in the military and was very regimented, so she was always expected to be very organized and follow the rules.

One of the challenges that Sarah had at work was her ability to see outside the box, to be creative. She did not see herself as creative and her upbringing supported the fact that she was led to believe that organization and regimentation was critical for success. Her prior beliefs, thus her view from Pluto, led her to believe she was not creative.

With that information, I was able to help Sarah to see how she in fact WAS creative, by seeing creative things she had done in a different light.

So take a trip to Pluto. Have dinner, stay a while, take in the sights. How do you want to change the way you communicate?

Now, go and change the . . . change Pluto!

The Hardest Lesson

What is the hardest lesson you have had to learn in your career and your life? We all have lessons to be learned in life, and some are more difficult to handle than others.

When you are coaching people, keep in mind that not all lessons are easy to learn. As a matter of fact, the best lessons learned are usually the hardest to learn. They take a great deal of thought and perseverance. As coach, it is our job to make sure that we give our people support as they experience these hardships. Make sure that we are giving them a pat on the back, putting some pep back in their step, and helping them to learn from the experience so they won't repeat it!

What would you say to someone who has just experienced their most difficult lesson? How would you keep them from snowballing into a spiral of negativity?

Use a PEP talk.

Positive attribute: What is a positive attribute you have seen in them, more than once, that you admire and WHY do you admire it?

Encourage: We all experience difficult times. This is how we learn. I know you will learn from this and become a better person for having had the experience.

Positive from the experience: What positive element, no matter how small, can you pull from this experience? Hint, it may be: this is how I will do it differently next time, so I never have to go through this experience again!

Be a great coach. Encourage your players. You all will reap the benefits.

Now, go and change the world.

BIRRR . . . Change Poor Behaviors

We've all been there. You have an employee who just doesn't get a certain behavior changed. This leads to a sub-standard performance in this area of their job. Substandard = unacceptable. Things have to change . . . and they have to change quickly. Your company's performance is being affected. What do you do? You BIRRR them.

BIRRR is a coaching method, five steps, that will help you to help them change their behavior. You cannot make them change their behavior, they have to want to do it. BIRRR can help give them the incentive they need to make the change.

Behavior: Call them aside (all coaching should be done 1 on 1, not in a group) and let them know you need to talk to them about a specific behavior. When you sit down with them, give them a specific time that you have experienced this behavior. BE VERY SPECIFIC about when and where you experienced this behavior.

Impact: Share with them the impact that this behavior is having on their performance, the team's performance and even the company's performance. Let them know how their behavior is impacting themselves and others in a negative way. Many times, they have not stopped to consider how their behavior is impacting things in a negative way. OUT OF SIGHT, OUT OF MIND.

Request: What is it you are asking them to do? Again, you cannot make them change their behavior, you can only help create an environment where they want to change their behavior. "What I am requesting is that you change your behavior." This is direct and to the point. "I am asking you to change your behavior." While it is direct, it is not dictatorial, it is still their choice. Give them two options to select from, two choices.

The first choice is to change their behavior to a specific behavior that you need to see them do.

The second option is for them to NOT change their behavior, for them to continue what they are doing. "What I am asking is for you to change your behavior to xxx. The other option is for you to not change, that is certainly your prerogative." Now they are empowered. Now it is their decision. You are giving them choices . . . YOUR choices. You still have the control here, while at the same time empowering them to move forward. Be SPECIFIC in what their options are.

Reward or Repercussion: You have given them two choices. Now it is time to outline the rewards for changing their behavior or the repercussions if they choose NOT to change the behavior. "If you choose to change your behavior to xxx, then the reward will be this" (list specific reward here. The reward must be something that is important to them. The reward must tie back to their current communication channel. See the blog on communication channels for a review). "If, however, you choose to NOT change your behavior, then the repercussion will be this" (list specific repercussion here. Again, this must be something that will be painful to them based on their communication channel).

Revisit: When you will revisit this performance/behavioral issue. Let them know there will be a follow up. This is the accountability piece. "We will revisit this issue on this date (give specific date and time here). When we get together to revisit this, the conversation will be based on your decision that you are making today on whether or not to change your behavior. You have the power to impact how that conversation will go and what will happen as a result of your decision."

BIRRR must be done in a direct fashion, in Driver mode. Be direct and take emotions out of the equation. This is strictly about behavior and performance. Be firm, let them know this is a serious issue and that you are on their side to help them correct the behavior. Let them know there is hope.

Practice this technique with someone you know and trust BEFORE you go and use it with an employee in a real situation. Remember, practice makes permanent. How you practice it is how you will perform it.

You can do it! Now, go and change the world!

BEHAVIOR
IMPACT
REQUEST
REWARD
REVISIT

Chapter 4:

ENGAGEMENT

Being engaged means that your head and heart are in the game. You care about the organization and what is happening. You feel like you are part of something bigger. You feel like you belong, like you are contributing.

Share Some PIE With Them

PIE is an acronym for a technique that gives honest positive feedback and shows appreciation.

Positive Attribute: What's a positive attribute you see in the person? When have you experience it recently? This is a very important part, providing evidence of the attribute.

Impact on Others: How did the attribute impact you, the team or the organization? Many people do not realize how their actions impact others in a positive way.

Encourage to Continue: Encourage the person to continue this behavior. "A behavior rewarded is a behavior repeated."

When you give someone honest, positive, evidence-driven feedback, it will improve your relationship and motivate the person to do that behavior more. For some, this technique will come easily. For others, it will take some practice. Ask them to share some PIE with others on the team. You will find your employees to be more engaged, more enlightened and more productive.

Now, go and change the world.

The Socratic Method

How much time to you spend putting out fires and solving problems?

50% or more? Stop solving your employees problems. Start HELPING them to solve their own problems. You hired them for their intelligence, so let's encourage them to use it.

The Socratic Method is this: Never tell them what you can ask them. With this method, you will notice that your people can solve lots of issues on their own. You can help them think it through and in the end, it is their idea. They become more empowered, more confident and more engaged. You have a more innovative and proactive work force, and you can spend more time doing what you need to be doing to move the team forward.

Now, go and change the world.

Give Gratitude

Gratitude is Golden. People need it, people want it. It costs you nothing, yet can provide an unbelievable amount of prosperity and good will. Find out what kind of gratitude is most important to them. Deliver the gratitude sincerely, regularly.

Here are the different types of gratitude. Find their favorite and mix it up from time to time. Keep it fresh, keep it real.

1. Verbal Words of Appreciation

What is something that you appreciate about THEM. Not about what they do . . . about them. Big difference. Value who they are, encourage them to be who they are more.

2. Pay it Forward

Go and do something for them. Do their job for 30 minutes, hold the door, get them a water, help them with a project. Do something nice for them to show them you appreciate them.

3. Pay Attention to Them

Give them some one on one attention. Spend some time with them. Ask them questions and then really listen to them. Show them you care about them by spending time with them. It really won't matter what you do, as long as you are focused on them.

4. Lagniappe

A little extra, a little gift. Give them something a little extra, a little gift.

5. Written Words of Appreciation

Write them a note, an email, a text message. Leave a post it note on their desk. Send them a letter at home. Write down what you appreciate about THEM . . . not what they do.

Now, go and change the world.

Exercise:

What is your favorite way to receive gratitude? Least favorite? Find out the same for someone on your team. Share ideas on giving and receiving gratitude.

Socratic COACHing

Are you familiar with term "constructive criticism?" It is an oxymoron.

When you criticize, you are being destructive. It puts most people on the defensive, so they are not as open to what you are suggesting---well ok, what you are telling them to do or do differently. It creates an irritation at best, and down right conflict at worst. What it does NOT do very well is change behavior.

Try this instead: Socratic Coaching. The great philosopher and teacher Socrates believed in helping people discover things for themselves. He believed in the saying, "Tell me and I will forget, show me and I will remember, involve me and I will understand." This technique is based on the Socratic Method, which is "Never tell them what you can ask them." Here is how it works:

Call them aside: Start by telling the person you want to coach that you would like to talk with him or her privately. Always do your coaching one on one. Tell her the purpose of why you want to meet with her, to talk about a specific performance or incident. This allows her to think about that particular performance and to be prepared for the conversation. So step one: Call the person aside.

Offer positivity: Offer him one positive thing that you liked about this particular performance. Be sure that you have some specific action that you saw, heard, or experienced him doing---the more specific the better. Also include why you liked this, what you saw the benefit to be for both him as well as for others. Step two: Offer one positive.

Ask questions: Ask her to share one positive thing that SHE liked about her performance. Make sure that she gives details and that she tells you the benefit of what she liked. Step three: Ask for one positive.

CALL THEM ASIDE
OFFER POSITIVITY
ASK QUESTIONS
CHANGE
HELP NEXT TIME

Change: Ask his what is one thing he will change the next time he does this activity that will make his performance even better. Again, specifics are important. He is, in essence, visualizing himself having a future success. He is planting seeds of success in his subconscious brain. Step four: One change next time.

Help next time: Ask her, as her coach, "What can I do to help you be successful with this change?" Let her tell you and then go out and make sure you do your part. This part of the coaching is building trust in your relationship; in fact it is building your partnership together. Step five: Ask what you can do to help next time.

You will realize that these five steps spell out the word COACH. Practice a few times and then put it to work. This is a very powerful technique that will serve you both very well.

Now, go and change the world.

We Buy From People We Trust

Who do you trust with your life? Nothing like starting out with a big question. And seriously, who is it you trust? This is a big question. Write down the names of the three people you trust most in this world.

Now, write down why you trust them. What is it, in your eyes, that makes them trustworthy? Your answers may vary. I am willing to guess that somewhere along the line, you wrote, or perhaps may add, that these people you trust the most are those you know the most, or they know you the most. Some of you will have answered

Exercise:

Write down the names of the three people you trust most in this world. Then write down why you trust them.

that you have been through some tough situations with them, down in the trenches as it were. Some will write that perhaps they are family, or perhaps they are people who you look up to for various reasons.

Now that you have your list of top reasons you trust someone, think about your relationship with your employees and the people you coach. Would you make their top three most trusted list? Why? Why not? In order to be a better coach, you must be more influential. In order to do that, you must build trust.

Before you coach your people to build trust, think about what is trust, from where does it come, and how can you build more of it. Also, what would the benefit of more trust be? My business partner and wife, Rachel, and I have been working on developing greater trust with one another since we started dating. We are always looking for articles, or classes, or books that will help us to challenge the status quo in our relationship, to help us open up and be more vulnerable . . . to share more of us with one another. It is working . . . MUCH greater trust between us which comes in handy daily . . . but it REALLY comes in handy when there is a stressful situation.

We buy from people we trust. You are a salesperson. Your people are your customers. How can you sell them your ideas and concepts better? Build more trust.

I would recommend you watch this video from Ted.com, by Brene Brown. **(http://www.ted.com/talks/brene_brown_on_ vulnerability.html)**

It is on vulnerability and trust. Watch it three times, then ask yourself, "What do I need to do to build greater trust with those who are important to me?"

Now, go and change the world by building greater trust!

The CHAT in the Hat

I love Dr. Seuss. Very clever, very simple, very positive, very fun. What if you could be more like Dr. Seuss in your coaching?

I don't mean that you have to start rhyming all of your coaching conversations, although that would be entertaining! I am talking about having an interesting, simple, effective, relaxed conversation . . . where it was a conversation, a sharing of information that was low key, informal and pleasant. Sounds good, doesn't it? Use the CHAT formula. Don't use all of the questions at once, just use one topic, one question at a time. Keep the conversations short (60 seconds) and concise. Keep them informal, ask opinions rather than facts. Get your people thinking, get some great feedback. Find out what they are thinking, so that you can help them reach their goals.

Clarify:
What results do we need?
What are the parameters?
Who is responsible?
What is the reward/repercussion?

Help:
What is it that you need to be focused on?
How can I help?
What is it you think I need to be more focused on?
How can you help?

Appreciate:
What is it you appreciate about your team?
What is it you appreciate about your teammates?
What is it you appreciate about yourself?

Appreciate your team: Pay it forward, PIE (Positive attribute you appreciate, Impact it is having, Encourage to continue); PEARL (written PIE), Face time (Spend time with them face to face), Lagniappe (from Parisian shoppe owners, a little something extra free of charge).

Thrive:

What are the things we need to start doing to improve?
What do we need to stop doing to improve?
What is broken? What needs to be replaced? What is outdated?

You now have a template to have a chat (maybe even wear a hat, think about that!) Go and have some casual conversations that can help you both to change the world, or at least your performances!

Now, go and change the world.

Mind the GAPPP

There are times when there is a GAP in performance, between what the desired results are and what the actual results end up being. When this happens, you need to have a discussion with them about the performance GAP that exists. I use this tool quite a bit. I was working with a client recently and we were talking about an employee, Rob, who was new and was learning how to do a new job. There were certain things that Rob did really well from the beginning---a natural! Then, there were some other things that Rob really tried and gave a great effort, yet he came up a bit short of the desired result.

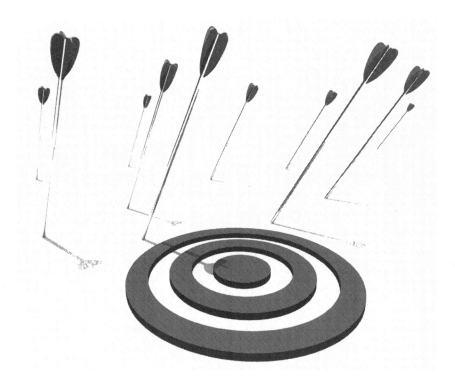

So we went and had a GAP discussion. It went really well. Rob left the meeting smiling and determined to hit the target the next time. Rob knew that his boss was in his corner, that he had his support and encouragement. Rob knew that he had fallen a bit short, but he had learned from it and was confident in trying again with a few alterations in how he would go about it the next time.

I am happy to say that Rob hit the target the next time. I believe it was due to the fact that Rob was confident and had a clear plan on how to achieve his target.

Here are the steps to GAP coaching:

Goal: The desired goal or output. Start with this, for example, "Rob, here is our desired goal, this is what we were striving to achieve."

Actual: The performance that the employee actually performed. "Rob, this is the result that you reached in this particular effort."

Particulars: What it is they did RIGHT in this performance, what it is that kept them from their desired outcome.

Possible solutions: What they can do next time to fix the GAPPP and hit the desired target.

Positive encouragement: Give them some positive encouragement, WHY you feel they will hit their target the next time. You now are ready to help people to bridge the GAPPP and improve performances!

Now, go and change the world . . . one GAPPP at a time.

Exercise:

What do you expect of yourself? What do want to aspire to? What areas need the most attention?

ENGAGE Tip #8:

Personal Pact

I was talking with a friend of mine recently about his job search. Bill was down on himself. He was middle aged and had tried what he loved to do, but he simply could not find a job that could support him and his family.

As I listened to Bill, I noticed a pattern in how he talked about himself. It was VERY negative. He berated himself all the time, far more than he built himself up. So I asked him if he was aware of this, and he told me he was not.

One of the things he said was, "I am not very smart." I said, "Bill, look at this job you had previously. You had to have a lot of intelligence to do that job, right?"

"Yep, you are right, Frank."

"So that tells me you are, in fact, intelligent, right?"

He looked at me with a glare, and then admitted that he, in fact, was intelligent. As we pursued this path, we found out that most of Bill's self-talk was negative and . . . a LIE.

How many of us LIE to ourselves? Bill had been in the Embrace Your Freakness experience and one of his Primary Values was integrity.

I pointed out that each time he lied to himself, he in fact was not being a person of integrity---with himself! He was not being honest with himself. So we sat down and wrote out a personal pact. This pact was about how Bill would interact with himself.

What things did he expect from himself? What things would he call himself on? We used the Team Charter form and adjusted it a tad. He made a pact with himself on what he would say, what he would do, what he would NOT say, and what he would NOT DO.

This was not a list of goals but rather a list of expectations and aspirations with HIMSELF.

A short time later, Bill and I got back together, and he assured me that he was in a much better place mentally and emotionally because he had stayed true to his personal pact.

Help your people to create a personal pact. Explain the concept, ask how you can help. Show them your personal pact. Ask them how they would like you to support them and their personal pact.

Now, go and change the world . . . one pact at a time.

ENGAGE Tip #9:

Synergy of the Season

Coaching is all about having synergy with your coachee. Synergy is defined as synchronized energy---you are moving in the same direction, in alignment with one another. What you do energizes them and their efforts and vice versa.

How do you create synergy? Here is a simple SYNERGY acronym to help you further develop synergy. GO through the seven steps. Which step do you need to focus on now? What can you do in one minute to improve that area of synergy? Keep it simple. Keep it short. Keep repeating.

Smile: You would be surprised how far a smile can go. Do you smile at your people? Do you give a positive facial recognition pattern (A smile) when they do something positive? Remember, behavior rewarded is behavior repeated. A smile is a very powerful tool and will help you to develop rapport and a stronger relationship.

eYe contact: Ok, I admit, a bit of a stretch for the acronym, but I had to make it work! Eye contact is important, especially in our western culture. Eye contact says, "Trust." No eye contact, no trust. Don't go over board and stare at them, but establish eye contact for 3 to 5 seconds. When you coach them, make sure to make direct eye contact. This step will help build trust with you coachees.

Name: Call them by their name. Dale Carnegie said that a person's name is, to him or her, the most important sound in any language. I believe that is true. Make sure to call them by their name, or a nickname if that is what they prefer. This shows that you care enough to know and use their name, that you do VALUE them.

Energy: Give them some positive energy, no matter what they are giving you. Ever watch the Dog Whisperer? Caesar always says that a dog, like a human, can sense positive or negative energy. He also says that you must be the Pack Leader. That means that you set the tone for the type of energy in the relationship.

Request: The best way to get someone to open up is to ask her some questions. Ask him questions about himself, about his opinions, her perspectives. Then listen.

Genuine: Be genuine in everything that you do with them. Don't do any of the above steps if having synergy is really not important to you.

whY: Without why, they don't buy. Make sure that when you talk to them, you talk about why. Why did this happen? Why did that not happen? Why is this important? Why should you do this? Without the why, you won't get buy-in from them. (Be sure to get them to tell you the why as often as possible; remember the Socratic Method).

This is a very simple tool, and it will help you to develop greater synergy and rapport with your coachees and employees.

Now, go and change the world.

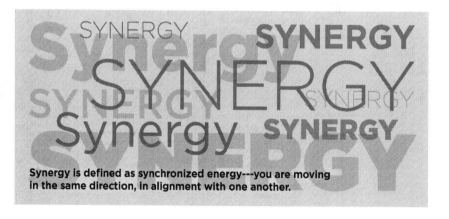

Synergy is defined as synchronized energy---you are moving in the same direction, in alignment with one another.

Goaled Check

You want your employees to be golden, right? Well, you can help them get there. As their coach, you want to help them to set some goals. Goal setting is very important, and that is usually where most support stops. We help them set goals, or perhaps set some goals for them, and then wait until next year and do the same thing over again.

It is the ongoing coaching that will help them to improve. Not nagging. Not cajoling. Coaching. Encouraging. Quizzing. Supporting.

I would suggest that when you set up goals, you also set up a frequency response. How often do you both want or feel like it would be best to get together to talk about these goals? Set this up for regular intervals. Discuss at the onset what these sessions will be like and how they would like you to best support them in achieving their goals. Some people will want these sessions to be very quick, "Here is what I have done; this is where I am. Goodbye." Others will want more encouragement. Some will want more feedback.

Regular support and feedback on goals is critical if you want your people to achieve their goals. They can be golden---and you can help.

Now, go and change the world.

The Focused Burst Technique

The Focused Burst Technique is a really simple and great idea. For those people who need to be focused (or if you need to focus), and you do not want to micromanage them, use this technique. The basics of this technique are as follows: Select an activity. Set a timer for 25 minutes, focus all of your efforts on that one activity for 25 minutes. Then go take a 5 minute break. This allows you to focus with greater intensity for shorter bursts of time. You then follow that burst of activity with a brain cool down, allowing for things to flow into your subconscious. You then start on another 25-minute activity. Set this up for your entire work day. Set a longer time consuming project into 25-minute compartments. It will help you to get more done in less time.

Now, go and change the world.

Create a Win/Win Situation

In order to truly be an aligned team with your employee or coachee, you must create win/win situations as much as possible. A win/win situation is where you both feel like you received something from the experience, from the exchange. So they get a win, you get a win. Sounds simple, doesn't it? Let me introduce you to a win/win template that is a tad different. It creates a traditional win/win situation while helping to improve communication and trust in the process. This is a simple formula to help you create win/win situations more often and ones that are more powerful and can help you both achieve more.

The first WIN is for What I Noticed. Share with them one thing you noticed that you appreciate. This helps to build their self esteem and lets them know you are looking out for them.

A second option of the first Win in Win/WIN is to share what-I-noticed-that-gets-under-my-skin, that drives me bonkers, that I have a problem with. This is tougher for most people. Think about this:

What kind of relationship do you have if you cannot be completely open and honest with one another? How much can you really help them if you have to be guarded all the time? This technique, while a bit uncomfortable the first time, is very powerful and a HUGE trust builder.

The second WIN is for What I Need. What is it you need from them? Be specific. Let them know what you need and why you need it.

Then have them do the same with you. Share their WIN/WIN. Sometimes it will be only one of you sharing. That is ok too. Be creative, how can this work best for you?

Now, go and change the world.

Chapter 5:

INNOVATE

Innovation is the ability to create new ideas, services, products and procedures to improve what we do and how we do it. The goal is to not only develop skills and abilities that lead to being innovative both professionally and personally, but also develop the mindset and culture in which innovation flourishes.

Pattern Interruption

When you hear the message on your TV, "We interrupt this program to bring you . . . ," it doesn't really matter what you were doing before the message started. It got your attention (of course, it also meant that whatever you WANTED to watch was probably not going to be on).

The concept is known as pattern interruption. You see, people TALK at an average of 150---200 words per minute. People LISTEN at an average rate of 800---1000 words per minute (you quite literally CANNOT talk too fast). What happens is that your brain, which is in constant need of stimulation, is bored. The words are coming in too slowly, so your mind meanders, if only briefly, and sometimes it comes back, sometimes it doesn't.

The problem is not people talking too fast, it is that the message becomes boring. Your brain is racing ahead. In order to keep your attention, I have to interrupt the pattern, the flow of information that is coming into your brain.

I can talk faster or slower, use a different language, move around the room, stop talking altogether, ask a question, change something physically in the room. All of these things will interrupt the pattern of information flowing into the brain and bring their attention back to our conversation.

I have found the most powerful way of interrupting patterns of others is by asking questions. When a question is asked, the brain hears it and must stop and figure out the answer. You might not talk out loud, but no matter, the damage is done---you have stopped your trip to another world and come back to our conversation via the question. I now have your brain engaged on what I want it to be engaged on. Very powerful tool.

Start using the pattern interruption technique when coaching your people. When you notice they are drifting away, seem to be glassy eyed, or just are not paying attention, throw in a question. It does not even have to be on the same topic! Just ask a question, then you can follow up with one that is on topic. Try different questions, try talking faster or slower, try changing the lighting in the room. Talk louder or whisper. Stop talking altogether. Find out what works with whom. Everyone will benefit from it.

Now go, Einstein was a genius, and change the world.

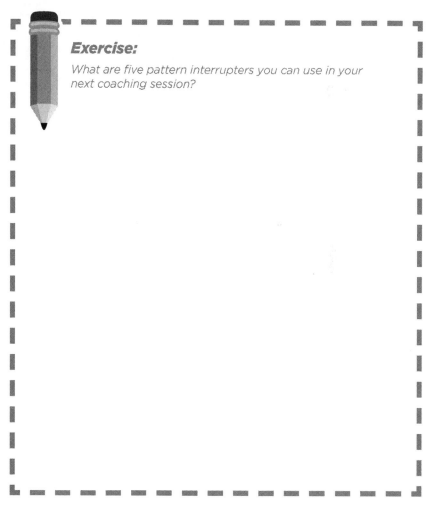

Exercise:

What are five pattern interrupters you can use in your next coaching session?

Mental Floss

You brush your teeth, don't you? Do you floss (according to the American Dental Association, only 50.5% of Americans floss daily)? You take care of your teeth, now it is time to take care of your brain and your people's brains. It is time to start flossing your brain.

When you floss your teeth, you are getting the old decay out of the areas between your teeth. Similar idea with your brain. Old ideas get stuck in your brain and decay your abilities to focus, be positive, and be objective. When you floss your brain, you will get rid of the old, yucky brain-plaque and have a cleaner, meaner brain.

How do you do it? It is quite simple really. Once an hour (during your waking, working hours) stop what you are doing and take a five minute mental break. This means to stop whatever work you are doing and go do something else, preferably something mindless. This allows your subconscious brain time to think about all of the input it has had in the past hour and time to do something with it. It allows your brain time to relax, to stretch, and to rest so that you are ready to go for the next hour.

Most of us only get one brain, so take care of it. Mental floss your brain once an hour. Give your brain the nutrients it wants and needs (most of us should drink a glass of water an hour to keep hydrated). Keep away from sugars and caffeine.

Here is a link to a great article on super brain food: **http://www.webmd.com/diet/features/eat-smart-healthier-brain** or **http://www.livestrong.com/article/326960-10-super-brain-foods-for-kids/**.

Now, go and lead a healthier, more alert and vivacious team . . . and change the world.

Three Ways to De-stress to Avoid Dis-stress

Build de-stressing exercises into your regular routine with your people, things that they can do to keep the stress at a minimum, and more importantly to learn how to deal with the stress that they do have in a positive way. You will find they have more energy, better brain power and greater stamina throughout the week by doing one-minute de-stressing exercises daily. Here are three ideas to get you going. Try these with your people, and make the necessary adjustments.

1. Take a mental break every hour. Your brain gets taxed. Give it a break. Once an hour, for five minutes, take a break from what you are doing. Go get some water, go talk to someone, listen to something funny, listen to some music. Do something completely different than what you were doing, and it will give your brain a break to keep it fresher longer.

2. Schedule energy filling activities. Stressful activities literally drain us of energy. Schedule throughout your day and week activities that you consider to be fun, positive and uplifting. Schedule these around any stressful events on your calendar. Set yourself up to keep your energy high at all times.

3. Eat chocolate and laugh, two of the best ways to bust stress. Build more of your bodies natural stress busters---ENDORPHINS. Endorphins are your body's way of dealing with stress at a chemical level. Endorphins give extra energy to your internal organs and your brain, so you have extra energy and stamina. The best ways to build extra endorphins are to eat some dark chocolate, to laugh, and add one more, vigorous exercise. Do one of these three times a day and see how much better able you are to handle stress.

Now, go and change the world.

Change One Thing

I was being coached by my boss at Circuit City one day. He had been writing everything down, and as we were wrapping up the coaching session, he asked me to sign the paper, stating that we had talked about ALL of these things. He handed me the paper, and I looked at it. It was FULL of items to fix or change. FULL, I tell you. So I signed it. Don't think I changed much on that list; it was so OVERWHELMING.

Stop overwhelming people, and instead help them to focus on ONE thing at a time. Just change one thing. What would that one thing be?

If you could change one thing that would have the most impact, what would that be?

Sometimes the thing that has the most impact is THE thing that is most likely for them to actually do---not perhaps the biggest, baddest, or best thing, but if they will do it and none of the others, well, then it is the thing that has the most impact.

Get into a habit of helping your people change ONE THING each day and before long, they will be unstoppable.

Now, go and change one thing in the world!

Stop overwhelming people, AND INSTEAD HELP THEM TO FOCUS ON ONE THING AT A TIME

INNOVATE Tip #5:
Listen to TED

Are you always looking for the next best thing? Do you like to get new ideas from some of the world's greatest thinkers? Then TED is what you need to know. TED is a website, www.ted.com and it is all videos. Thousands of them, on all kinds of subjects. Math, science, reading, leadership, space, bees, the brain, smiling, listening---you name it. There is most likely a talk by someone BRILLIANT on the subject. It is a nearly endless supply of really cool and interesting ideas that can help you to keep things fresh and interesting for your people. Have a one minute coaching session talking about a TED talk. Share with your people the TED talk you want them to watch, then have a conversation about it. Start with your 60-second coaching conversation and don't stop there if they want to talk more. You will find these talks do really stimulate conversation and creativity.

Now, go and change the world . . . and let TED help you do it.

Five Caps Thinking

Many perspectives, to be more precise . . . .When most of us begin problem solving, we look at things from one perspective, our own. In order to get the best solution for your problem, in order to get the best ideas for innovation, you must see things from multiple perspectives. See things from multiple perspectives with Five Caps Thinking. Five Caps Thinking stretches you beyond your own perspective (thus out of your own mind) into four other perspectives, seeing the problem/idea in new ways. You most likely will have to do some research, do some digging, and make an effort to find other perspectives. The simplest way is to involve other people in the brainstorming process. Ask their opinion, ask them for advice, ask them how they see the issue. Select five different perspectives (each perspective represents a cap). You can do more than five if need be, but five is a good place to start.

When I do innovation and problem-solving workshops, I take the participants through a Five Caps exercise. Here's the gist of the exercise:

1. Put your group in a standing circle.

2. Start brainstorming by going around the circle making suggestions and coming up with ideas. One person, outside the circle, writes down the ideas for the group.

3. After a few minutes, add the Five Caps element.

4. Have all the participants in the circle put on the first cap (the first perspective). Brainstorm possible solutions/ideas for a few minutes (3-5 minutes gets the ideas out, gives a set amount of time, and usually after three minutes people are ready for the next cap). Again, write down all the input.

5. Go to the second cap (the second perspective) and gather ideas. Repeat this process until you have brainstormed using all of the perspectives. You'll find this gives you many ideas that you would not have thought of from a single perspective.

This same exercise can be used when digging down to determine root causes. Look at the problem from five different perspectives. What questions would each perspective ask?

Now, go and change the world.

Practice Being Illogical

Logic is drawn from things that make sense to you. What makes sense to you? Things that fit an existing pattern in your brain. So if it fits a pattern in your brain from existing information, then you can draw a conclusion from it. But what if we want to be creative? What if we want to think outside the box? What if we want incredible, fresh, new ideas? Then logic many times---most of the time---will not work. You need information or thoughts that you have NOT had before. You need to create new patterns. This is a function of your creative brain, your right brain.

By practicing thinking things that do not fit an existing pattern, you are coming up with new ideas, fresh ideas. You are also being illogical. I am NOT saying ALWAYS be illogical. I am saying do some creative thinking with your employees. Get their brains out of the doldrums. Set a time each week to come up with new ideas. Teach them how to think differently---it is a skill, I believe.

For your 60-second coaching on this, sit down with your employee and give him or her one Mind Puzzle or Lateral Thinking Puzzle. You can Google either term and find many puzzles of each type on the internet. Give your employee the puzzle and one minute to figure it out. Give clues to help out. After one minute, if he does not have the answer, give it to him. Talk about the experience: What did he like? How could he do better next time? Offer suggestions you might have for him. Then do another one next week.

I like the saying, "If you'll always do what you've always done, you will always get what you've always gotten." I have added to it, "If you'll always go where you've always gone (in your brain too), then you always be where you've always been."

Now, go and change the world . . . by being a bit silly and a bit illogical!

INNOVATE Tip #8:

Brainflood: 60 Second Brainstorming

How would you like your people to have better, more creative ideas? Help them to develop a creative thinking habit. One such technique to help them develop a creative thinking habit is the Brainflood. This is brainstorming in 60 seconds. Draw one shape on a piece of paper---I would suggest these shapes: do one each time you brainflood and then repeat the shapes: circle, square, triangle, star, rectangle, octagon, hexagon, oval, quadrilateral, cloud, starburst, line. Then come up with as many things as you can think of that this item can be in one minute. Write them down. Keep track of how many items you come up with. This will help you start to stretch your creative capabilities.

As you repeat each object, not only keep track of how many, but also of what you come up with. Challenge yourselves to come up with new and more eccentric ideas.

This WILL help you to get outside of your brain box.

Now, go and change the world by changing how you think.

The Opposite

You have heard the saying that opposites attract. That is true in many relationship situations. There is an attraction with something or someone who is different, who has a different perspective, who can offer something you did not see yourself. She can offer you something you don't have. This works in creative thinking circles too.

When you need to get out of the box and generate some new and improved ideas, think of the Opposite. Here is how this works: Think of ten things that you know about the situation. Then write down the opposite of each of those ten things. This will help get you started in seeing things from a different perspective.

When coaching your people, ask the opposite questions. What would happen if you did the opposite? Two things will happen here (maybe more): First, you will get them thinking about the situation, so bingo! You are teaching them to think out of the box. Second, they just might come up with something cool or unexpected. They might figure out something that has kept them from moving to the next level, they might see something, however small, that helps them take a big step forward. So try the opposite from time to time. What would the opposite of that be? How would that work?

Now, go and change the world.

Puzzled? You Should be to get Better Results

Are you puzzled? You should be. Puzzles help your brain to stretch, to see things differently. Puzzles are a good tool to use to help develop the creativity in you and your people's minds.

What kinds of puzzles help creativity? Here are but a few:

Crossword Puzzles: They are good at making you think of things in a little bit different way.

Sudoku: Maddening perhaps, but they help you to think of numbers in ways you do not normally think of them.

Lateral Thinking puzzles: They help you to see things differently, to develop your lateral thinking abilities (not your logic).

Mind Puzzles: They help you to look at things (visual images, pictures) and see things a second way, a different perspective.

Do different types of puzzles each week with your people, five to ten minutes a day, and you will see significant improvement in their ability to be creative.

Follow the links to some puzzles to get your minds going.

Crossword Puzzles: http://puzzles.usatoday.com/, http://www.boatloadpuzzles.com/playcrossword,

Sudoku Puzzles: http://www.websudoku.com/

Lateral Thinking Puzzles: http://www.rinkworks.com/brainfood/p/latreal1.shtml

Mind Picture Puzzles: http://www.funnyjunk.com/funny_pictures/98196/Brain/

Now, go and change the world by being puzzled.

INNOVATE Tip #11:

Innovate, Create, Don't Wait

By asking this question, you can get your people to start being more innovative. Being innovative is a state of mind.

The more you encourage it, the more they will be innovative. Start with this question. Ask it several times each week: "What is one thing we can do to improve our team?"

Then sit back and listen, really listen. What does their answer tell you? Do they have an answer? If not, why not? If so, find out more about it. How would they go about doing it? How would they propose you pay for it? Who would do it? Dig a bit deeper. The soil will be richer. The growth will be greater.

Now go and change the world.

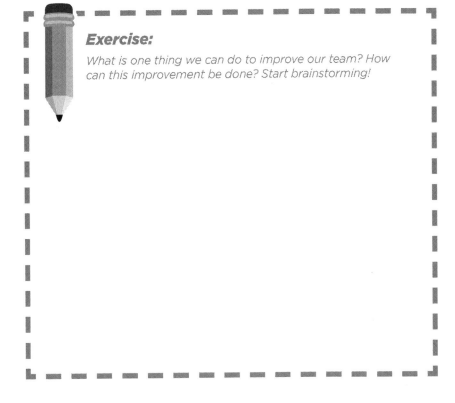

Exercise:

What is one thing we can do to improve our team? How can this improvement be done? Start brainstorming!

Recharge YOUR Batteries

This one's for you! As a coach, you are always giving, giving, giving. In order to keep on giving, and not deplete yourself, you have to recharge your own batteries.

Here are a few ideas on how to recharge your own batteries:

1. Make a list of the top 5 things in life that energize you, that make you feel great. We call this your Energizers List.

2. Set specific times during your day to do as many of these things as possible from your Energizers List.

3. Make a list of things that deplete you. Make sure that when you have a scheduled depleter, you schedule an energizing event before AND after the depleting event.

4. Review your Mental Mints. Keep your brain fresh. Review your Mental Mints, review your Driving Force and your Values.

There you go, a few quick hits that will help you to recharge your batteries on the run.

Now, go and change the world . . . with RENEWED energy.

INNOVATE Tip #13:

Take a Mental Vacation

Remember that song from the '80s group, Frankie Goes to Hollywood? "Relax." Great advice. Relax. Many managers are really good at getting their people to become tense, stressed, overworked perhaps. How often do we as leaders take time to tell our people to relax and take a load off? Taking a mental vacation is so very important. Not a two-week hibernation of your brain, mind you, just a one-minute-rest-your-brain-think-about-something-fun-and-relaxing mental vacation!

If you encourage your people to do this once per hour at a minimum, you will find that they have greater stamina throughout the day. You will also find they are in a better mood as the day goes along, and they GET MORE DONE usually with BETTER RESULTS. Take Frankie's advice, coach your people to "relax, don't do it." Rest your brain, have some fun, then jump right back into it!

Now go and change the world . . . and relax while you do it.

Epilogue

You have worked through the entire 60-Second Coach book. By now, you see the benefits of knowing your people better---at a deeper level---knowing yourself at a deeper level, and developing deeper and more effective relationships.

The goal of this book has been to help you get to know your people better, to get to know yourself better, and to increase the performance of your people and, perhaps, of yourself.

First, you learned their CORE, their Driving Force and their Primary Values. This helps to understand what's important to them so you can better help them be motivated and help them increase their desire to lead a better life and be more productive at work.

Second, you and your people set some goals, i. e., where do you want to end up? (As Steven Covey said in his book *7 Habits* . . ., "Begin with the end in mind".)

Third, you started to develop greater clarity, greater understanding of one another and how each of you thinks, responds, and communicates.

Fourth, you then helped your people become more engaged in life (and at work). Mentally and emotionally, they started to invest themselves into WHAT you and the organization are doing and WHY you are doing it. It is usually in this stage that we start to really notice an increase in our people's personal motivation and determination.

Finally, you helped them become more innovative, to always be thinking about how we can do things better, faster, cheaper. Changing your beliefs from the status quo is okay but it's merely a step along the way. Let's find the NEXT level of greatness.

Thanks for your involvement in the life and betterment of your people. You are creating your legacy, and things will never again be the same as what they were.

My challenge to you now is to keep challenging yourself.

How can you keep your growth pattern in tact?

How can you keep your people growing and striving for optimal performance?

Made in the USA
San Bernardino, CA
19 July 2015